Jobs People Do

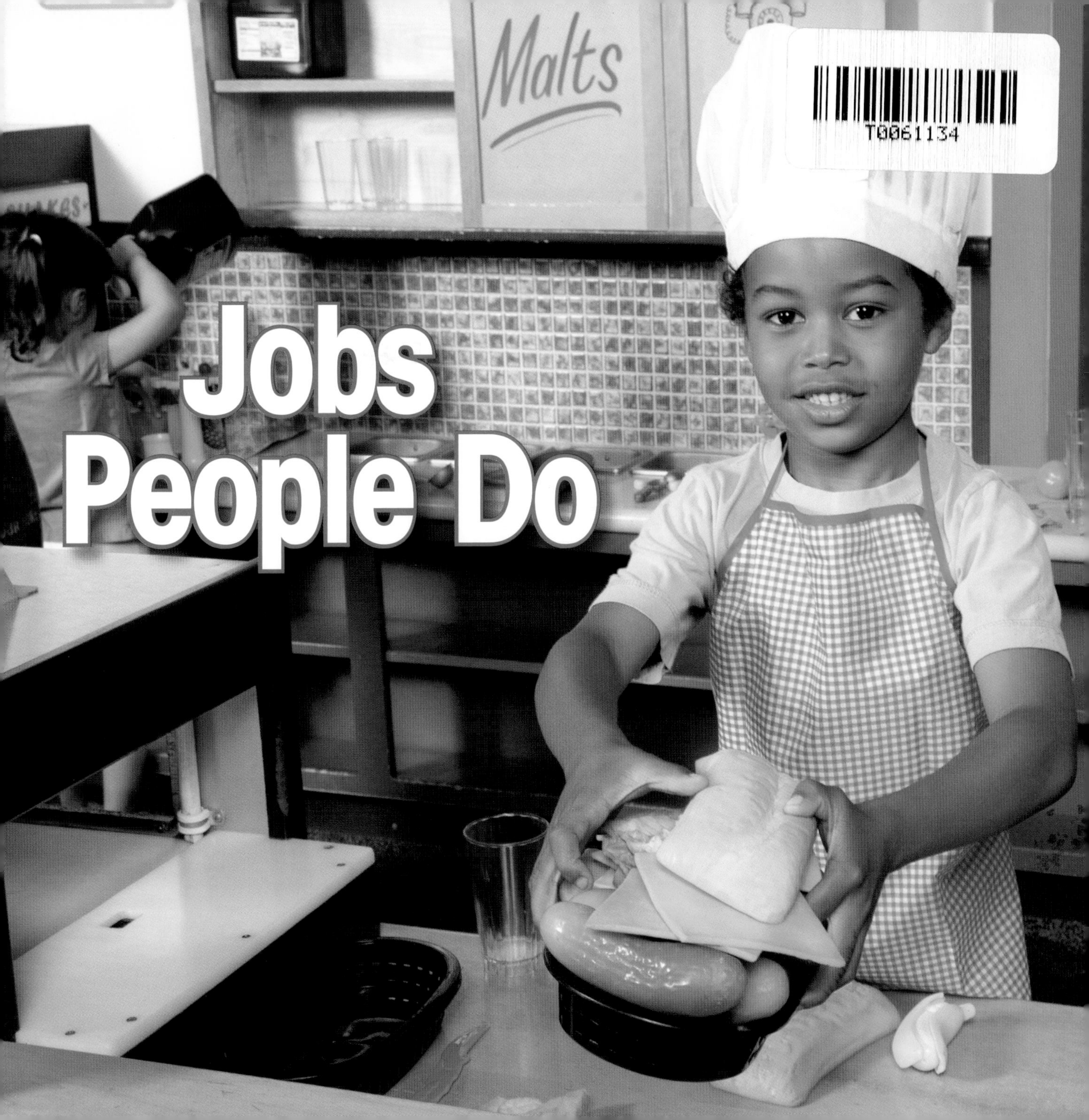

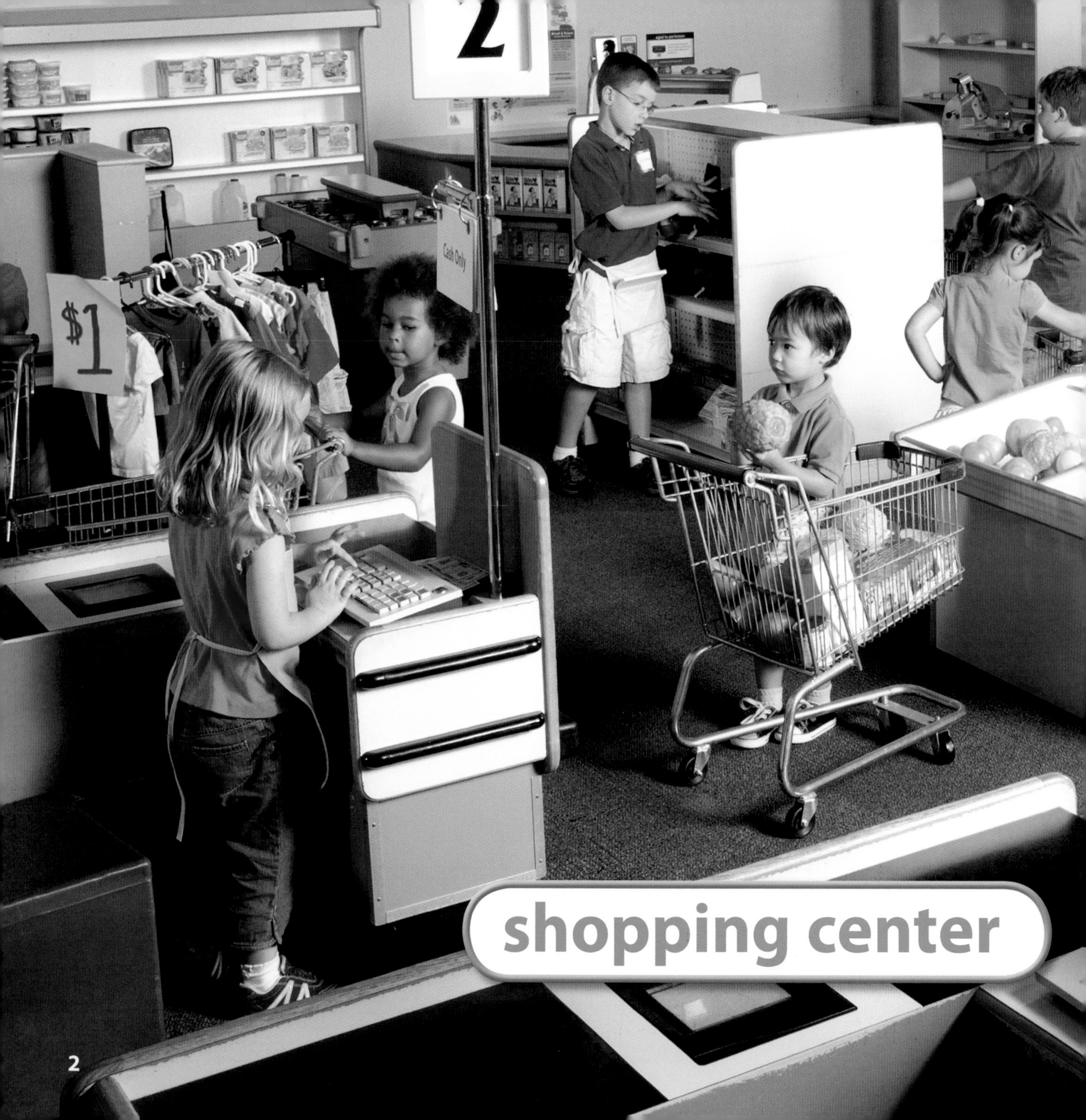

shopping center

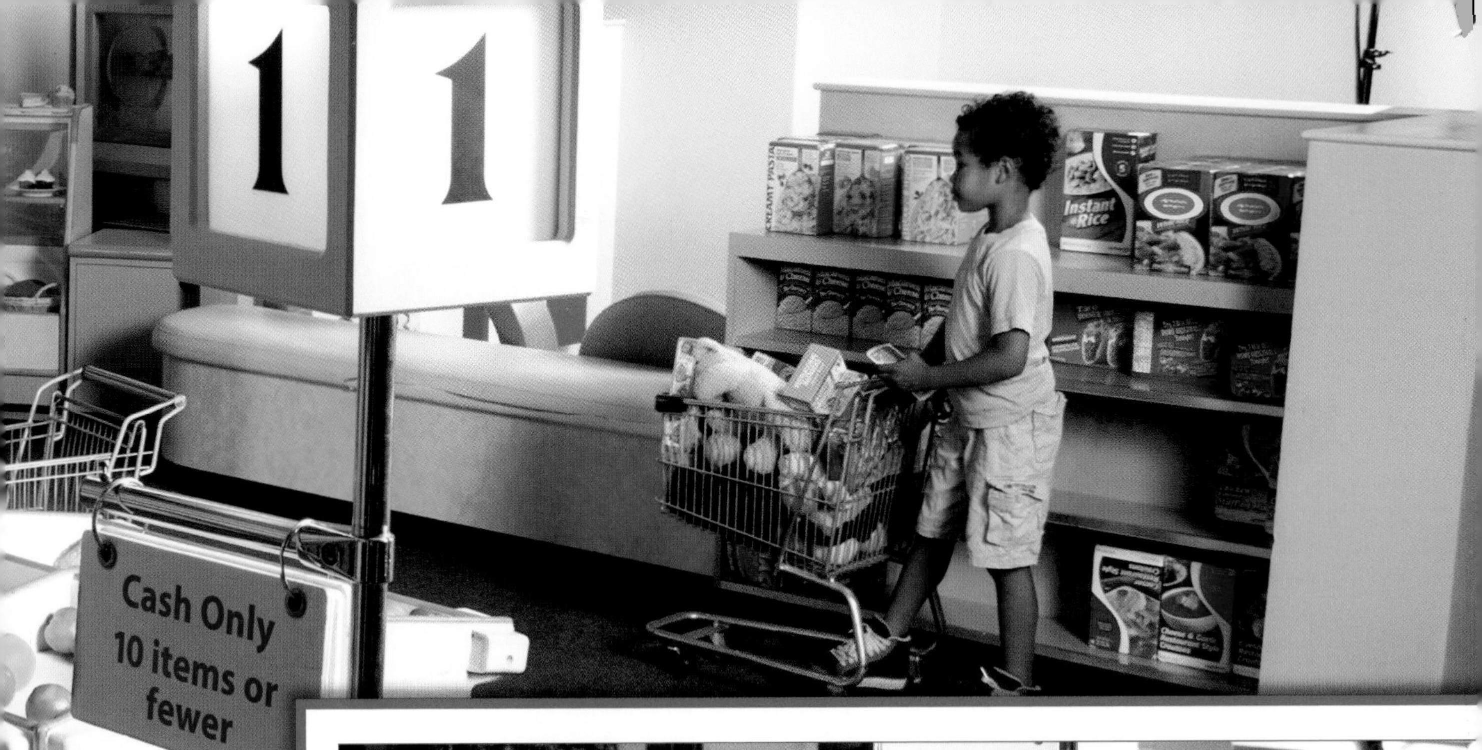
1
1
Cash Only
10 items or
fewer

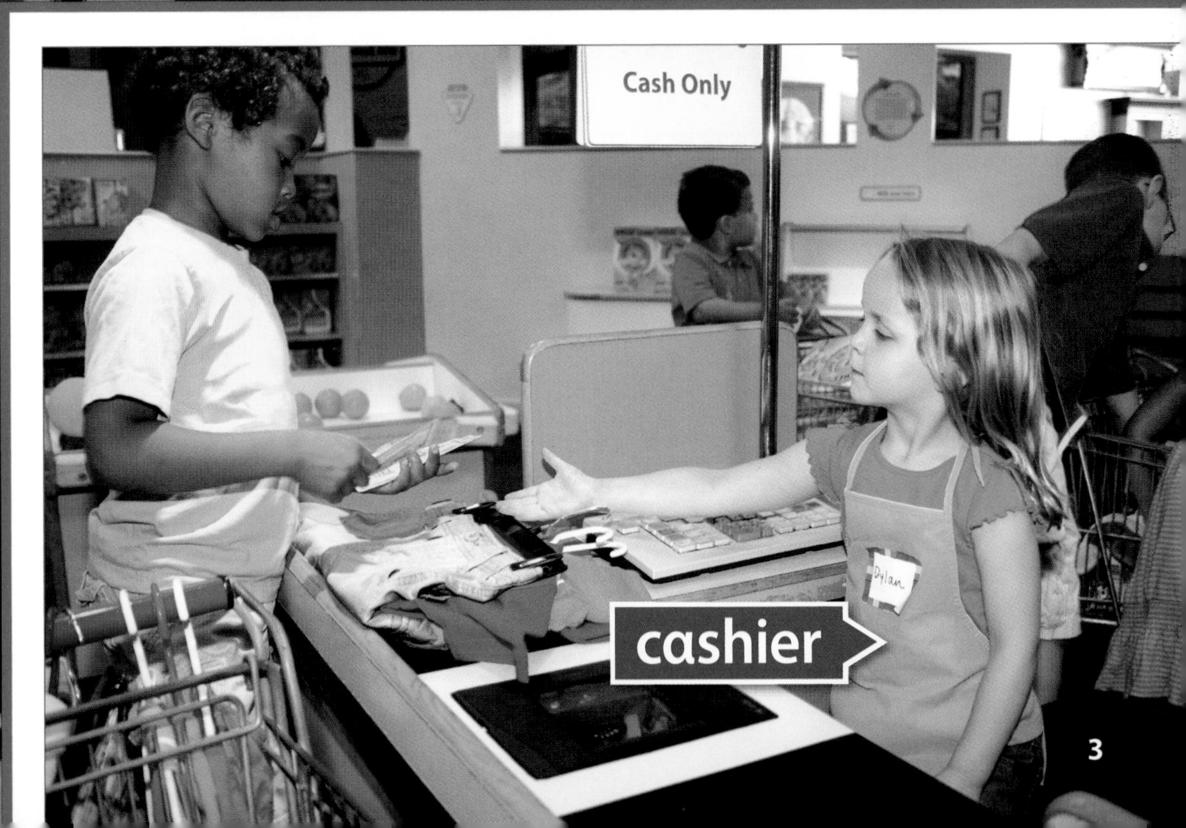
Cash Only
cashier

hospital

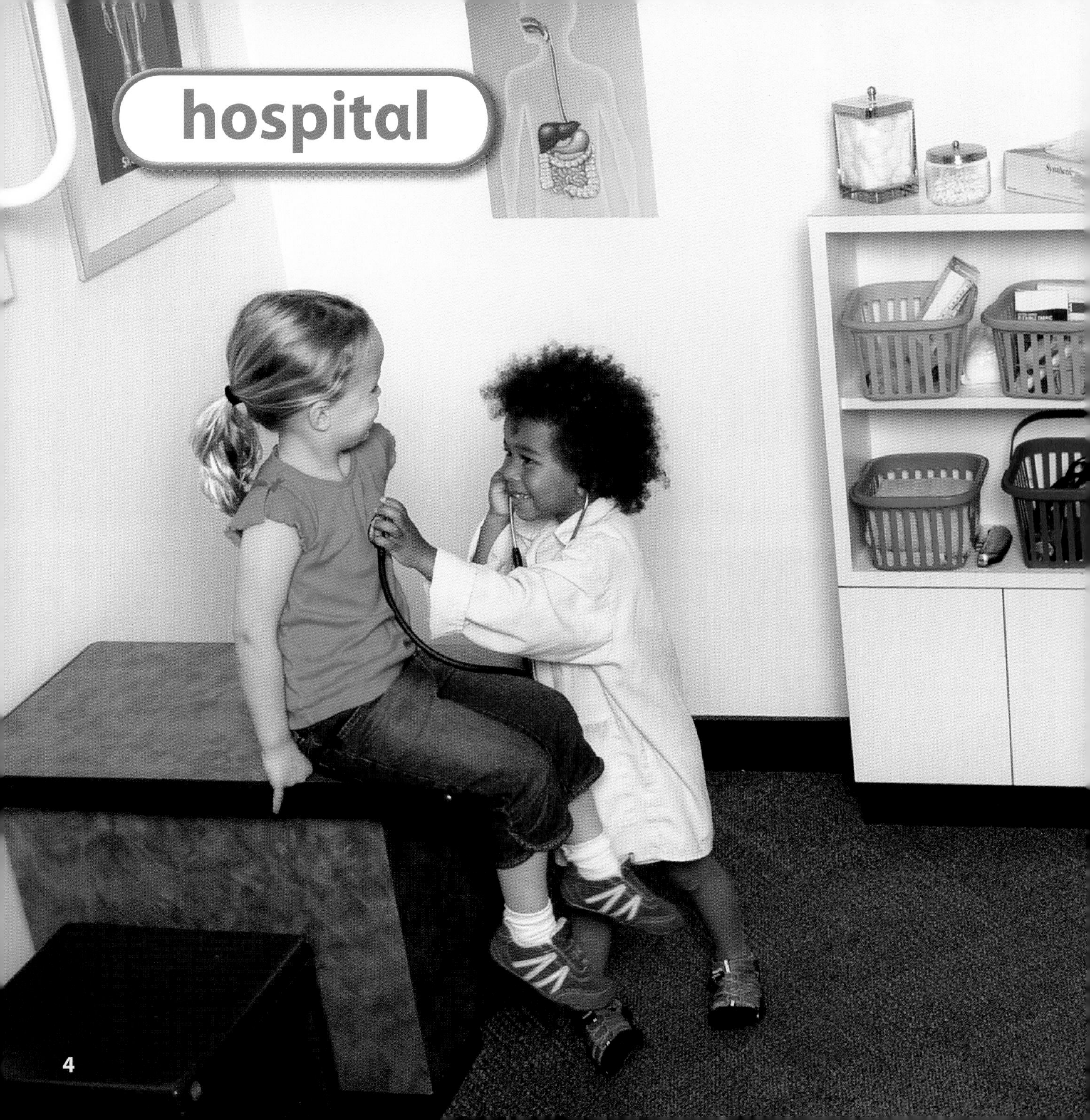

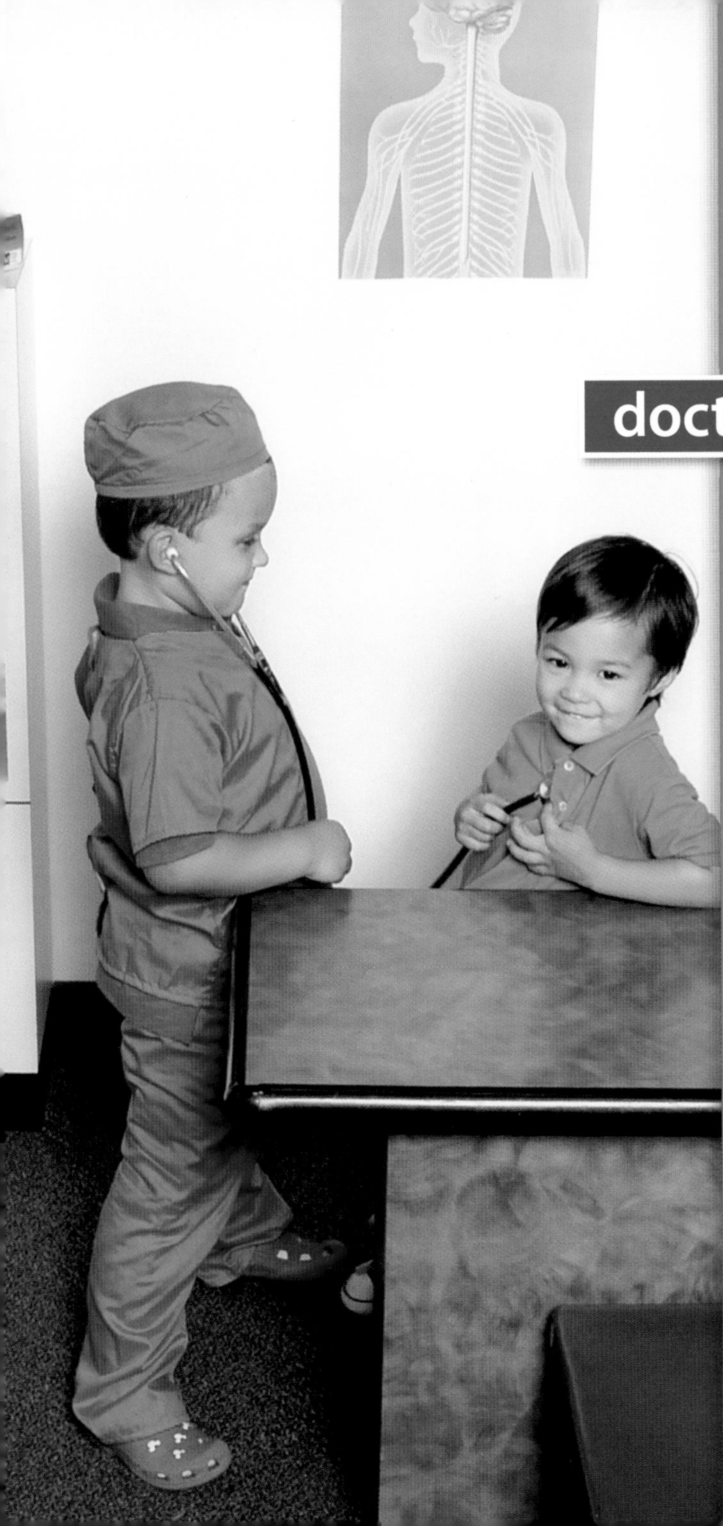

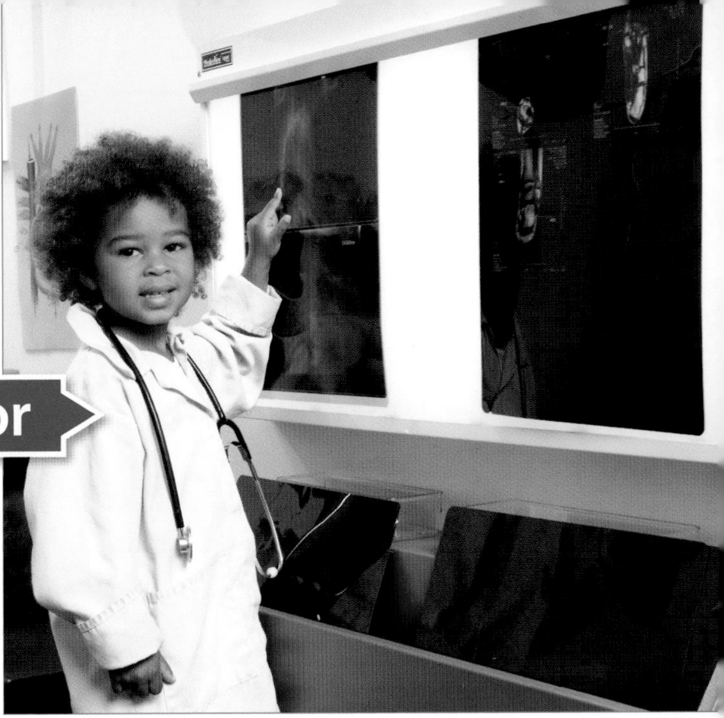
doctor

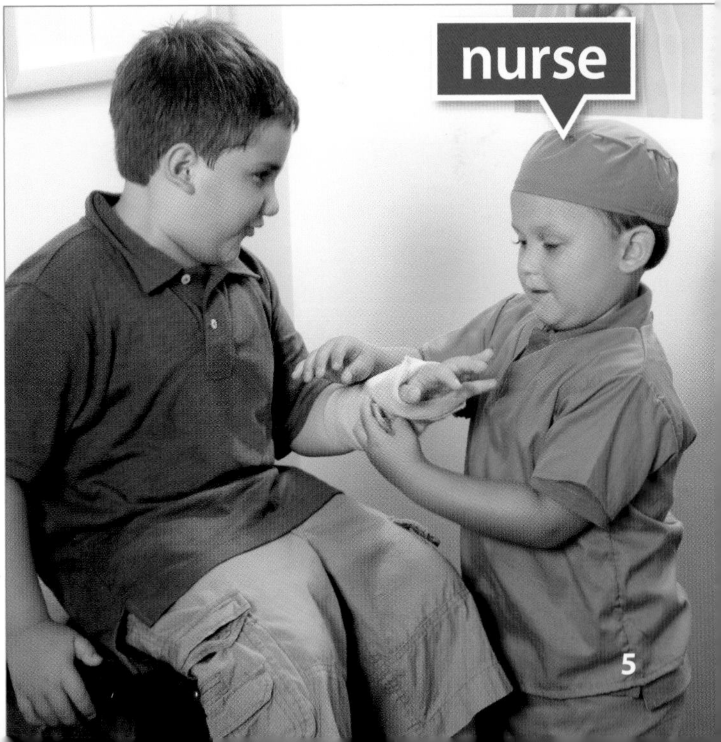
nurse

restaurant

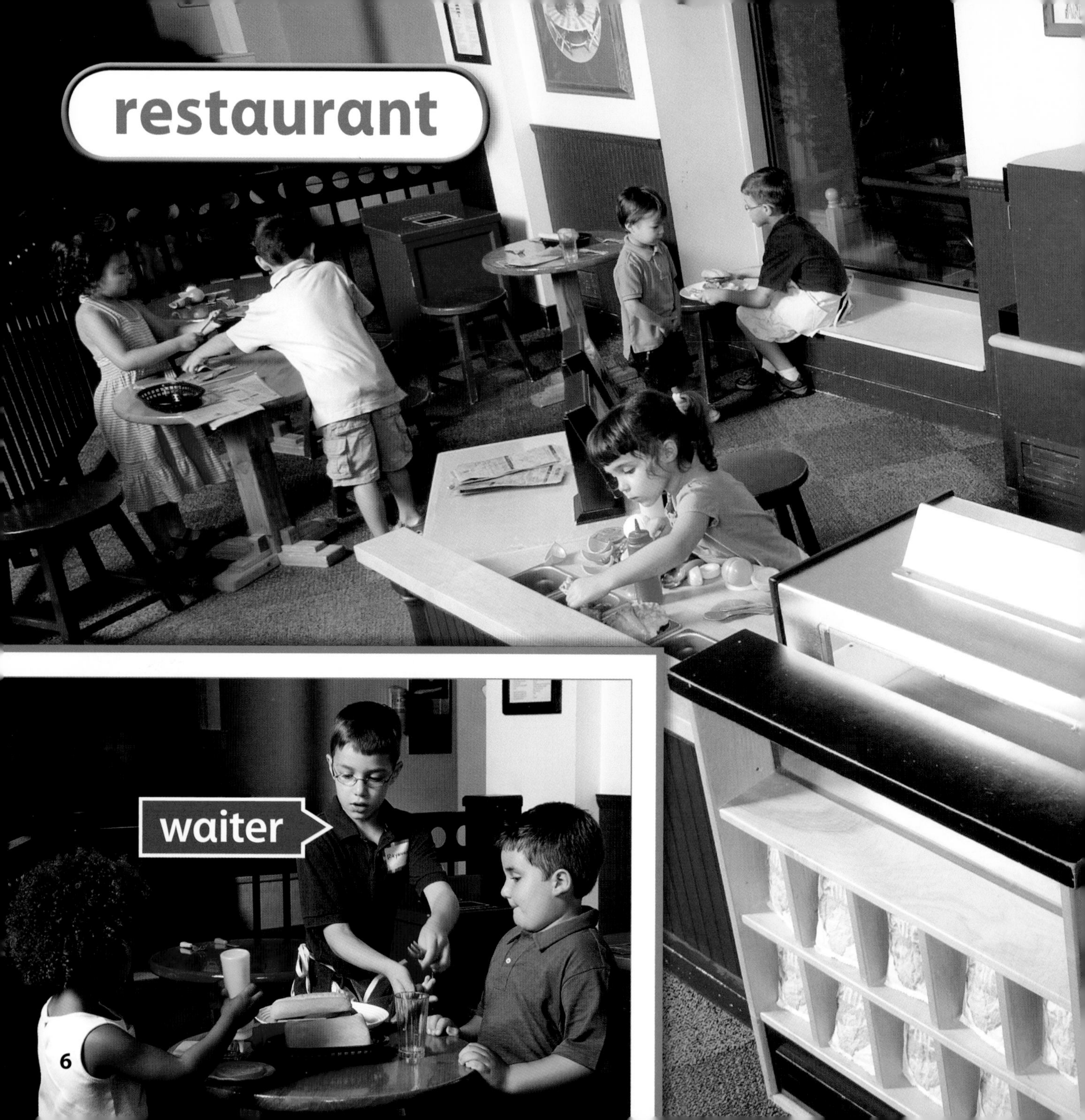

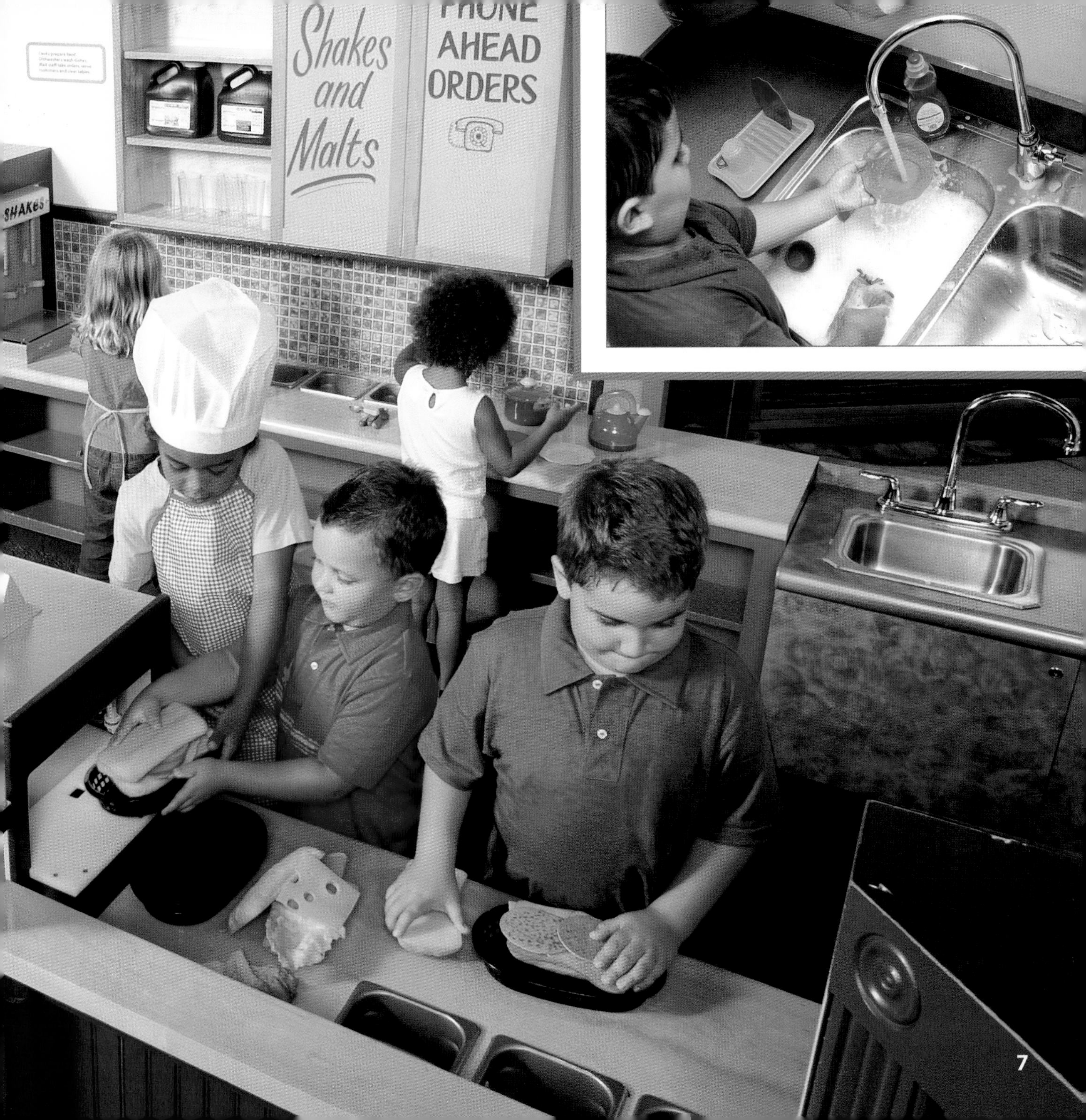
SHAKES
Shakes and Malts
PHONE AHEAD ORDERS

I want to be a . . .

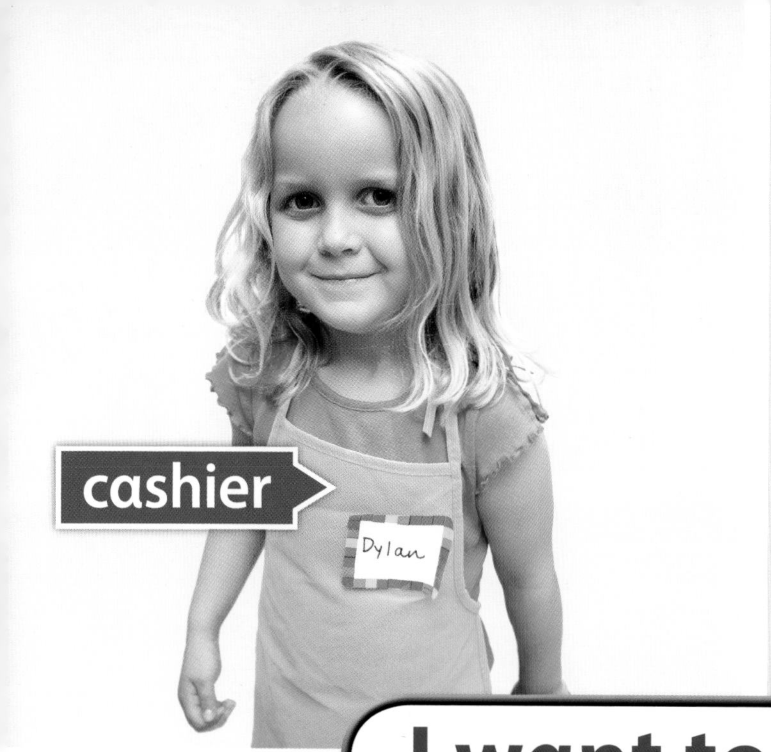

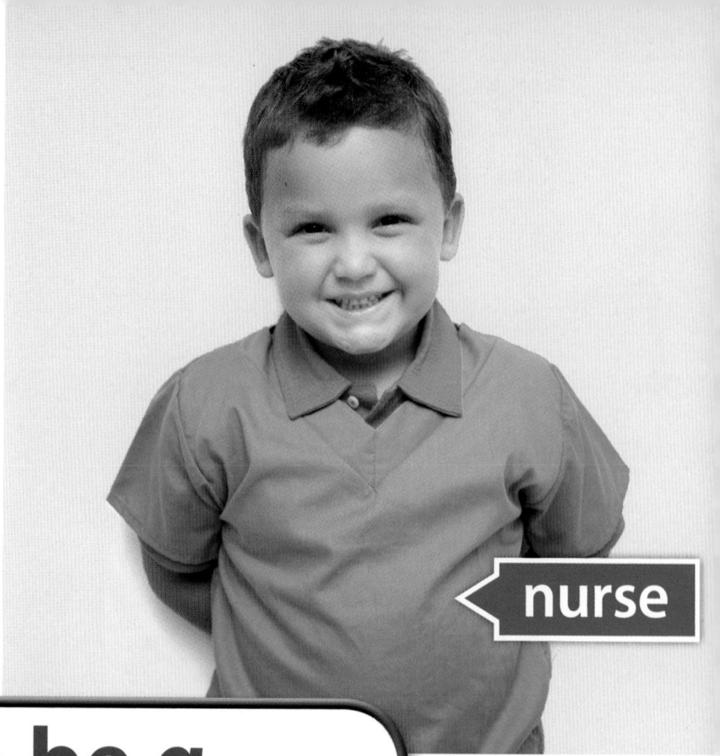

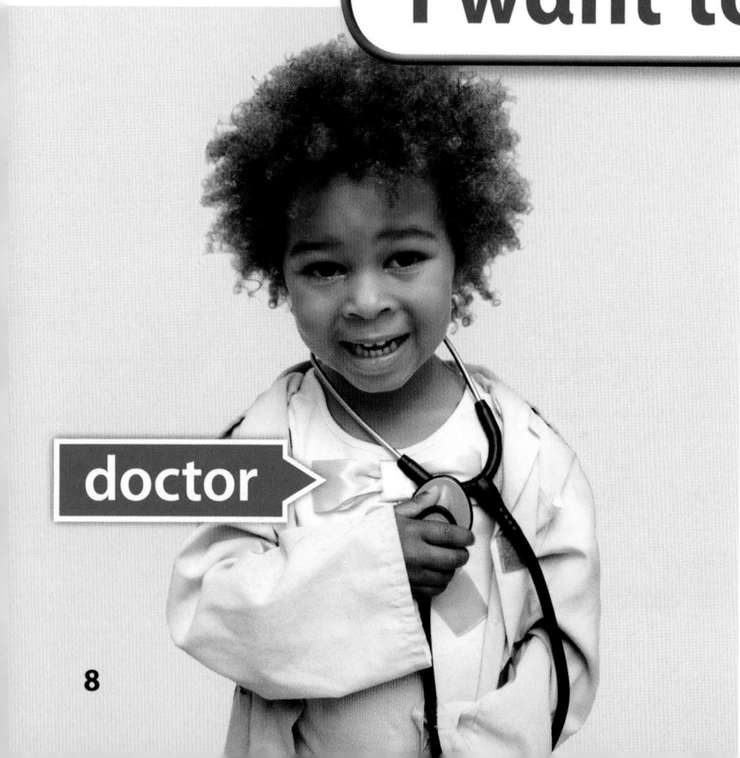

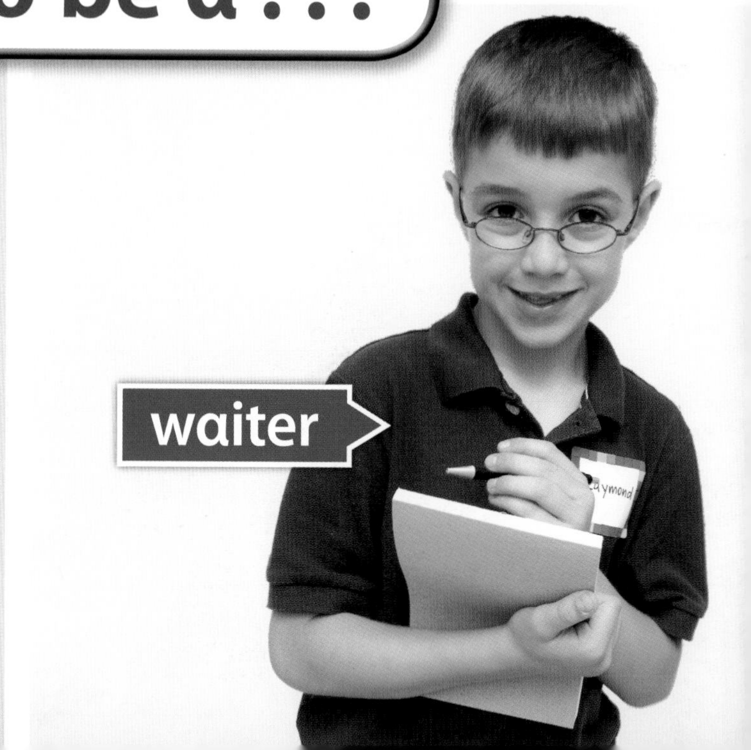